RESEARCH PRIORITIES IN NORTH-EAST INDIA

(WITH SPECIAL REFERENCE TO MANIPUR)

Editor
LUCY ZEHOL

Regency Publications
NEW DELHI

Division of
DAYA PUBLISHING HOUSE
4760-61/23, Ansari Road,
Darya Ganj, New Delhi - 110 002
Phone: 23245578, 23244987; Fax: (011) 23260116
E-mail: info@regency-books.com
Website: www.regencybooks.com

ISBN 81-87498-39-0

Published by Regency Publications, 20/36-G, Old Market, West Patel Nagar, New Delhi 110 008 and printed at Radiant Printers, New Delhi, Phones: 574 0038, 571 2539; Telefax: 578 3571

Email: regency@satyam.net.in

Foreword

Research Priorities in Social Sciences in Manipur largely results from the panel discussion held on October 28, 1993. It was sponsored by the Indian Council of Social Science Research—North-Eastern Regional Centre, Shillong, and organised by Prof. R.P. Singh, Department of Geography, Manupur University, Imphal in association with the Imphal Chapter of Indian Institute of Public Administration. Several scholars from the concerned disciplines and others including administrators were invited and participated in the panel discussion.

Panel discussion on Research Priorities was purely an academic exercise to know from the scholars in different parts of the North-East about the areas covered adequately or not at all covered in Social Sciences. Some of the scholars invited presented short papers at the panel discussion indicating the priority areas. Scholars approach a topic as they understand it, and the understanding is dependent on their making background and attitude. Some of it finds expression in source of them.

I take this opportunity to thank Prof. R.P. Singh and all his friends and colleagues who contributed papers and participated in the panel discussion. I also thank Dr. Lucy Zehol for going through the papers and editing them. Dr. C.J. Thomas, to be thanked for all the personal interest he took in the Research Priorities.

I hope that this small work will be found useful by those interested in north east India, more particularly Manipur.

Shillong
July, 2001

Jai Prakash Singh
Ex. Hon. Director,
ICSSR-NERC

Foreword

Research Priorities in Social Sciences in Manipur largely results from the panel discussion held on October 23, 1997. It was sponsored by the Indian Council of Social Science Research—North Eastern Regional Centre, Shillong and organised by Prof. R.P. Singh, Department of Geography, Manipur University, Imphal in association with the Imphal Chapter of Indian Institute of Public Administration. Several scholars from the concerned disciplines and others including administrators were invited and participated in the panel discussion.

Panel discussion on Research Priorities was purely an academic exercise to know from the scholars in different parts of the North-East about the areas covered adequately or not at all covered in Social Sciences. Some of the scholars invited presented short papers at the panel discussion indicating the priority areas. Scholars approach a topic as they understand it and the understanding is dependent on their making background and attitude. Some of it finds expression in some of them.

I take this opportunity to thank Prof. R.P. Singh and his friends and colleagues who contributed papers and participated in the panel discussion. I also thank Dr. Dev Zehol for going through the papers and editing them. Dr. C.J. Thomas is to be thanked for all the personal interest he took in the Research Priorities.

I hope that this small work will be found useful by those interested in north-east India, more particularly Manipur.

Shillong,
July, 2001

J.B. [illegible]
Ex-Hon. Director,
ICSSR-NERC

Contents

Foreword iii
List of Contributors vii

Introduction: *Lucy Zehol* 1

Chapter 1 Basic Issues and Resource Guidelines 10
A.K. Ray
Chapter 2 Political Approach 16
Bimola Devi
Chapter 3 Geographical Approach 20
R.N.P. Sinha
Chapter 4 Determining Research Priorities in Manipur 25
R.K. Ranjan Singh
Chapter 5 Physiographical Approach 28
N. Ram Singh
Chapter 6 Historical Perspective 31
G.P. Singh
Chapter 7 Environmental Research 35
Asha Gupta
Chapter 8 Export Potential of Manipur Handloom Products and its Economic Implications for the State 39
V.S. Pai
Chapter 9 Research Priorities—Economics (I) 41
E. Bijoy Kumar Singh
Chapter 10 Research Priorities—Economics (II) 47
Y.S. Singh
Chapter 11 Recommendations 51

List of Contributors

1. Asok Kumar Ray
   Department of Political Science, Presidency College, Motbung.
2. Bimola Devi
   Department of Political Science, Manipur University.
3. R.N.P. Sinha
   Department of Geography, Manipur University.
4. R.K. Ranjan Singh
   Manipur University.
5. N. Ram Singh
   Department of Agricultural Economics, Manipur Agricultural College.
6. G.P. Singh
   Department of History, Manipur University.
7. Asha Gupta
   Department of Life Sciences, Manipur University.
8. V.S. Pai
   Department of Commerce, Manipur University.
9. Bijoy Kumar Singh
   Department of Economics, Manipur University.
10. Y.S. Singh
    Directorate of Planning, Government of Manipur.

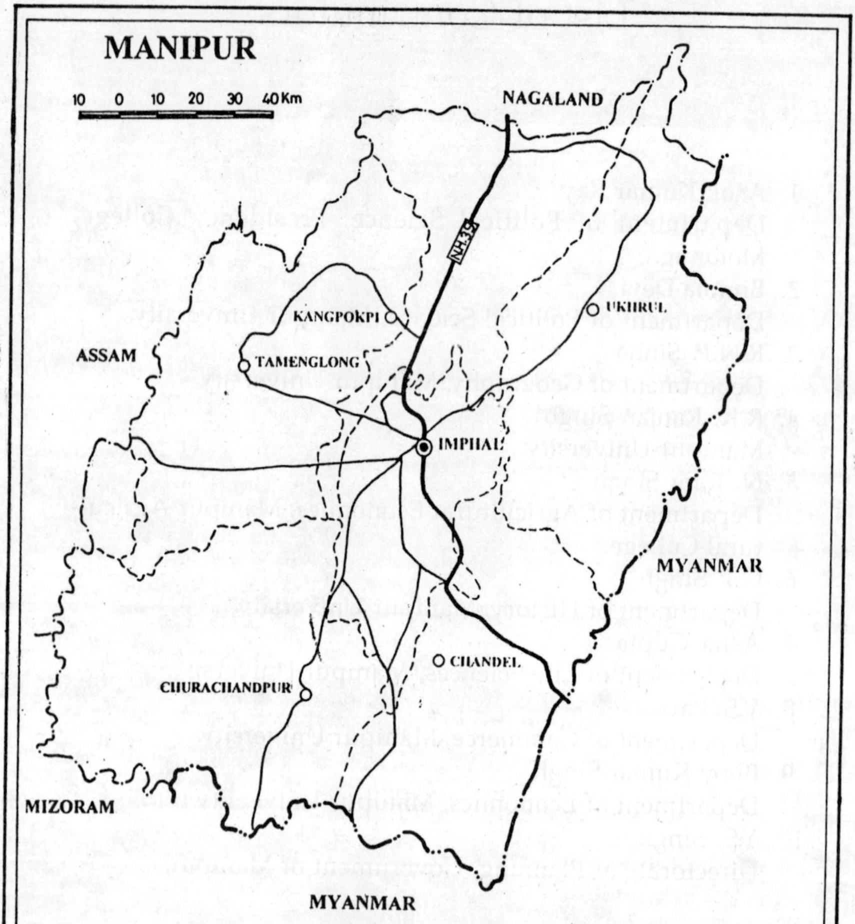

MANIPUR
10 0 10 20 30 40Km
NAGALAND
NH39
UKHRUL
KANGPOKPI
TAMENGLONG
ASSAM
IMPHAL
MYANMAR
CHANDEL
CHURACHANDPUR
MIZORAM
MYANMAR

Introduction

I

North-Eastern Region of India, has seven political units namely Arunachal Pradesh, Assam, Manipur, Meghalaya, Mizoram, Nagaland and Tripura.

The region bears a great deal of geographical, linguistic, social, cultural, religious and economic heterogeneity. The geographers and Human ecologists speak of some five major topographical units covering North-Eastern region. These are the plain areas of Assam, Manipur and Tripura, river valleys of Arunachal Pradesh, Plateaus of Meghalaya, Hilly areas of Nagaland, Manipur and Mizoram and the Higher Mountain found in Arunachal Pradesh.

In terms of linguistic families and sub-families the North-Eastern region has three major Linguistic Zones namely the Indo-Aryan, the Austric and the Tibeto-Burman. Racially, most of the tribal population of the North-Eastern region is of Mongoloid origin. The Australoids, it is reported were followed by the Mongoloids after whom came the Caucasoids. The religious heterogeneity also characterizes the North-Eastern region. The tribals are Christian in general, Buddhists and animists while Non-tribal population in this region follows predominantly the Hindu faith. Economically, the region as a whole is very backward. In transport and communication also, the level of development is far from satisfactory.

The region has multi ethnic groups of people. Added to all the above mentioned features of the North-East, one can also mention the long history of openness of the region to alien influence, and instances of fast changes in the socio-cultural and religious life of the people.

II

Manipur is located in the extreme eastern part of India. A small tip of southern Manipur adjoins Mizoram. It's other neighbours are Nagaland in the North and the Cachar district of Assam in the west, the North Cachar Hills of Assam in the south east. Like the other states in the North-East, Manipur too has its international borders with Myanmar in the south and the east.

Among the seven sister states of the North-East India (Assam, Arunachal Pradesh, Meghalaya, Mizoram, Nagaland, and Tripura), Manipur in many ways is distinct from other states for the following reasons:

Manipur is the home of the now famous Manipuri classical Raslila dance. It is also known for the famous and beautiful Manipuri handloom products. Manipur is the land of the legendary Ranı Gaidenliu. Moreover, during the Second World War, besides Nagaland, Manipur was part of the country which witnessed the march of the Japanese forces, subsequently, converting it into venue of war. Much prior to this, before the British rule in India, Manipur had been twice captured by the Burmese. In other words, Manipur has been the venue of many wars. After Independence, Manipur has been the scenes of some of the worst forms of insurgencies. Ethnic situations is undoubtedly the worst of its kind in the present decade. Last but not the least, the population of Manipur is unique, it has two distinct category of tribal and non-tribal population. What is distinct about this is that, it is only in Manipur that there is rather a very sharp and distinct cultural differences between the two sections of the population. Compared to this in Assam and Tripura, both of which also have "mixed population" like Manipur, there is much of culture transfer between the tribal and the non-tribal sections of the population.

The topography of Manipur comprises of two geographical regions. The valley and the surrounding hills. The hills of Manipur are the abode of the different tribes inhabiting the state. The hills comprises of nearly 90 percent of the total area of the state, while the tribal population inhabiting it account for nearly 27.30 percent of the total population of the state. In other words, more than that of 70% of the total population of the state is concentrated in the 10 percent of the land of the state i.e., the Imphal valley. This is the abode of the Meiteis who accounts for nearly 60 percent of the total population of the state.

Manipur is ethnically heterogeneous. The people inhabiting Manipur can be divided into two broad categories—the tribal communities and the non-tribal communities. In terms of distinct ethnic identity the people in Manipur can be broadly classified into four distinct groups:

(i) the Meiteis, including the Loi (Scheduled Castes)
(ii) the Bishnupriyas
(iii) the Pangans (Manipuri Muslims) and
(iv) the hill tribes

The Meiteis are the main inhabitants of the valley. The Imphal valley and the Meiteis are usually taken as synonymous. The Loi scheduled castes are scattered throughout the valley, interspersed with the Meiteis. The Bishnupriyas are concentrated in some villages around Bishnupur. The Manipur Muslims, locally referred to as the Pangans, are to be found mainly on the fertile tracts of land between the Imphal river and the Iril river. The tribes inhabiting Manipur are concentrated in the hills with some tribal pockets in the valley.

The tribes inhabiting Manipur can be divided into two broad groups—the tribes belonging to the Naga group, and the tribes belonging to the non-Naga group.

Officially, the tribes of Manipur have been classified into three groups:

(i) The Naga group of tribes
(ii) The Chin-Kuki-Mizo group of tribes and
(iii) The intermediary category of tribes, i.e., which strictly speaking, undecidedly traces linkage of identity with both the major groups.

According to official recognition (Directorate of Tribal Welfare and Backward Classes, Manipur, 1981.) the total number of tribes and their names in each of the groups are as follows:

(i) Naga group of tribes
Kabui (Rongmei and Puimei), Kacha Naga (Liangmei and Zemei) collectively known as Zeliangrong, Moa, Maram, Tangkhul and Maring.

(ii) Chin-Kuki-Mizo group of tribes
Gangte, Hmar, Lushai (Mizo), Paite, Simte, Thadou (Kuki), Vaiphei and Zou.

(iii) Intermediary group of tribes
Aimol, Chiru, Koireng, Kom (collectively called Komrem), Anal, Chothe, Lamkang, Koirao/Thangal, Purum, Mongsang and Moyon.

III

Keeping in mind the above background of the region and while reviewing the researches in the historical and contemporary context, it can be observed that a lot more remains to be done.

In the beginning British administrators, missionaries, travelers and others wrote about the life and culture of the people of this region. More so over the years scholars from India and abroad have made their contribution along with some administrators and defense officers.

A review of the research contributions suggests that

(1) There is a need for more monograph on ethnographic accounts of communities of this region.
(2) Many of the tribes/non-tribes are yet to be studied in a holistic perspective.
(3) There is a need of professionally trained local scholars to work on their own tribe or society.
(4) The need of restudy over a period of time either by the same scholar or others to understand the dynamics of change.
(5) While collecting data, one should also explore the principles governing each society.
(6) Last, but not the least, is the need for more empirical studies.

In other words, Research priorities in the North-East have to be a mixture of descriptive, analytic and explanatory studies. There are significant differences between descriptive, analytic and explanatory studies. The presence of this difference should not be taken to imply that there is no significant inter-relationship between these three types of studies.

In fact, descriptive research forms the basis for the other two categories of research. Similarly no explanatory research is possible without available analytical accounts. Descriptive research comprise of an arranged presentation in terms of the units of the phenomena. In case it is a study of say a village, a descriptive account of the village will comprise of information about the units as location, environment, population, land types, economy of the people, social and religious life of the people, the political organisation of the village, material and non-material communication of the village with its neighbour etc.

Analytic research are descriptive research plus an analysis of the inter-relation between the different units, as for example, education and political organization. Analytic studies focus attention on the nature of behaviour of one unit with relation to change in the characteristic of the other unit. Analytic studies with references to descriptive studies, extend and include analysis of pattern of change between two or more than two related units.

Explanatory studies/Research extends beyond where analytic studies stop. In explanatory research, the focus of attention is not only to outline the trend of relationship (analysis) but also outline causal analysis which deals with questions like: if this (cause) then that (effect) the effort is to explain the change.

We believe that our task is not to offer solution or provide an answer to the various problems we face today but to add a little more to our knowledge of human society and culture to better understand some of these problems.

Understanding North-East India in general, and Manipur in particular, is a challenging task for all of us. Let us take up this challenge with fortitude.

IV

The papers brought together in this book were presented at a panel discussion on "Research priorities in the North-East for the 90s" organised by Prof. R.P. Singh, Department of Geography, Manipur University, in collaboration with the Imphal Chapter of Indian Institute of Public Administration, and Indian Council of Social Science Research, North-Eastern Regional Centre, Shillong on 28th October 1993. Several academicians, administrators, students and others actively participated in the panel discussion.

The papers are arranged here serially as per the sequence of academic sessions.

A.K. Ray in his paper 'Basic Issues and Resource Guidelines' covers the research priority areas in Social Sciences more particularly in socio-economic and political fields relating to Manipur. While dealing with the primary source materials preserved in the different archives of India, he highlights the nature and contents of the archival records preserved in the National Archive of India at Delhi, West Bengal Archive at Calcutta, and the Archives at Shillong, Guwahati and Imphal. Not only this, he also refers to secondary source material preserved in different institutions. He also refers to valuable documents published so far as source material useful for the purpose of carrying out researches on different aspects of history and culture of Manipur and other neighbouring States.

Bimola Devi in her paper on research priorities 'A Political Approach' stressed the need for undertaking further researches on the interaction between traditional political institutions of the tribal people of Manipur and modern political institutions, role of voluntary organisations in the politics of the State, working of political parties both at the national and regional level, role of women in the socio-economic and political life in Manipuri Society.

R.N.P. Sinha in his paper 'Geographical Approach' emphasises the need of undertaking extensive and intensive researches for planned development at various levels—village, block and district, on quality of life, hierarchy of settlements both rural and urban, rural settlement patterns, land use, particularly in the tribal areas, administrative boundaries, impact of planning process on the socio-economic life of the people and its impact on environment, etc. He covers all aspects in a wide perspective in the context of the entire region.

R.K. Ranjan Singh, in his paper 'Determining Research Priorities in Manipur' stressed the need of carrying out further investigation into various problems related to development and progress of the State. The research priority areas covered by him encompass the following—the effect of traditional jhum cultivation on land and forest, low productivity of land, land use and problems associated with it, under the prevailing climatic and physiographic conditions, food habits of the people, changes in the cropping or farming pattern of the State, particularly in the hills, problem of introduction and implementation of natural farming technique, the impact of environmental upheavals or uncertainties in the social context, various economic programmes for hills as well as valley, etc. He laid special emphasis on the foothill zone of the State, which is normally neglected in any type of study or research.

N. Ram Singh deals with developmental research in his paper entitled 'Physiographical Approach' and emphasises on the need for studying physiographic characteristics like altitude, climate, soils and environmental endowments which provide necessary backdrop for developmental planning of an area. The research priority areas suggested by him included water harvesting, agricultural production and productivity, rural technology, power and energy resources, and flora and fauna of the State.

G.P. Singh discusses Research Priority in a 'Historical Perspective' and stresses upon the need for carrying out further researches on the origin, ethnology of the tribal people along scientific lines with the help of all available sources. He also pointed out towards undertaking archaeological explorations and excavations for rediscovering the past. The research priority areas outlined by him embrace all the three periods of history—ancient, medieval and modern and cover the political and cultural contacts of the people. The rise and growth of Hinduism and Buddhism, tribal republics, internal and external trade and commerce, the role of the tribal people in frustrating the repeated attempts of the Muslims for subduing them and thereby extending their authority, tribal renaissance and reform movements, anti-British movements, etc.

Asha Gupta in her paper priorities in 'Environmental Research' highlighting the multi-disciplinary nature of environmental sciences laid stress on the need for local initiative for undertaking collaborative research projects of three categories—(i) Based on local needs like low cost sanitation, both urban and rural, non-conventional energy resources etc., (ii) Based on community needs like disposal and recycling of waste, flood management and water pollution, and (iii) Theoretical and experimental studies that need long monitoring like conservation of fragile ecosystems, impact of development actions (dam, hydro-electric projects in the hilly areas) on environment and settlements. She specially mentioned in this category conservation, management and improvement of wild-life with particular reference to Sangai, animal-plant relationships and growing ecosystems.

V.S. Pai in his paper 'Export Potential of Manipuri Handloom Products and its Economic Implications for the State' touched upon the handloom products of Manipur with special reference to their export potential for the domestic as well as external markets. He underlined the importance of indigenous cottage industries in the socio-economic set-up of the State and also identifies areas to be researched.

E. Bijoy Kumar Singh in his paper 'Research Priorities—Economics (I)' emphasised the need for adopting an inter-disciplinary approach for the study of the resource bases of the region, for formulating development plans with the help of appropriate technology, for demographic studies and the studies about shifting cultivation and its impact on environment. He also stressed the need for adopting technological innovations in the field of agricultural development and for accelerating all-round growth of the state economy.

Y.S. Singh, discusses 'Research Priorities—Economics (II)' in agricultural and industrial development of Manipur. The priority areas for further researches suggested by him include: (a) Physical resources of the region, (b) Land use pattern, (c) Planning process, (d) Performance of public sector undertakings, (e) Industrial potential, and (f) Power, transport, communications, etc.

Although the authors have not adopted uniform methodology, their concern for research priorities for the state of Manipur comes up well in their presentations.

I hope this book will inspire and help scholars and others who are interested in this region. I wish to thank all the contributors and ICSSR, Shillong particularly Dr. C.J. Thomas for making this monograph possible.

Lucy Zehol

CHAPTER 1

Basic Issues and Resource Guidelines

In the sociology of underdevelopment the choice of research priorities is a pedagogic risk. A totalistic view on an underdeveloped society is that the whole society is a unit of urgent research and as no aspect of the society is discrete and isolated, all are structurally connected with one another, there can be no area which *per-se* may claim priority. Nevertheless there are certain areas which in term of degree are more exposed than the others, as a symptom of social pathology and so those areas may deserve the benefit of priority.

We have three levels to assess priority in social science research.

At the first level, the priority areas are decided on the basis of purpose and goal, i.e., either for administrative purpose or for the purpose of initiating a change in the desired directions. The former is a short term and the latter is a long term goal. It is here that obvious goal conflict emerges.

At the second level there is a hiatus between the pragmatists and the determinists in the selection of areas of research priority. The former emphasises on those areas and issues, which are surfaced, more perceptible and require immediate research attention .The latter on the other hand, tends to go into the basics of the socio- pathological exposures and go for a process analysis. So even when the pragmatists and the determinists take up the same issue the treatment differs. The former makes an insular study and the latter adds dimensions, and it is these dimensions that get priority.

At the third level, the Action Sociology demands extrication from the maze of theories and concepts and draws attention on urgent problems and their solutions. The priority is attached to those areas, which can redress grievances, minimise exploitation and ensure social and economic justice within the framework of under developed societies.

We can reduce the whole debate into a few basic questions:

1) Whether priority should be given to issues or to concepts,
2) Whether short-term implication or long-term implication should be taken into consideration for deciding on priority,
3) Whether should we give priority to situational problems without correlating them with structural phenomenon?

Keeping in view the above basic questions, let us go on identifying some of the areas of social science research.

On Manipur, the initial emphasis was laid on ethnographic and anthropological studies. By 1960s there was a large number of ethnographic and anthropological literature in print (Needham). By now this literature has been quite enriched.

But on the other hand, from 1960s onward the political developments make us to shift the attention on politico-historical studies. This development matured in the 1970s and 1980s, so much so that an academic break through in this field has become necessary. From the dawn of Independence not less than twenty para-political and political groups came up from the tribal society of Manipur with demands for multiple type of hill autonomy. Some of these are:

1. Demand for a separate Federal State,
2. Demand for separate Revenue District,
3. Demand for Union Territory,
4. Demand for the 6th Schedule of the Constitution,
5. Demand for 'Autonomous State',
6. Demand for Inter-State tribal integration,
7. Demand for trans-territorial integration, etc.

In the valley, the movement for Statehood (in 1960s) and the language movement came up. The latter got momentum in the recent past. Hitherto a princely state, Manipur's merger with the federation in India has invited a mixed reaction in the recent political researches in the field.

In the economic field the following areas deserve research priority.

1. Land Reforms
2. Tenancy Reforms
3. Land Reforms and Cadastral Survey in the hills.
4. Reassessment of the tribal land ownership system ,
5. Viability of Jhum Cultivation.

In the socio-cultural field the following are important.

1. To reassess the credibility of the traditional institutions and customary laws *vis-à-vis* modern institutions and State laws.
2. To examine the status of languages.
3. Folklore studies.

These are some of the areas in different fields of Social Sciences which need further research.

In the 1990s the main thrust of research should be on reassessment, and on the inter-disciplinary dimensions. The field wise identification of the priorities in research areas is made only for functional purpose. Emphasis may be laid on the three basic questions that are paused above. As check notes, we should take care of two aspects—relevance and purpose, otherwise the selection of priority areas will become meaningless.

GUIDELINE ON RESOURCES

Archival Resources: The Manipur State Archive, though young, has become quite rich in its collection. There are revenue records, political files, administrative reports, boundary records, darbar proceedings, etc. The Record Section of the Manipur Secretariat is also an important source of archival records. The National Archive of India preserve the Manipur papers (1825–1834). The Miscellaneous Records of the Foreign Department including Survey Reports of the Eastern Frontier. Report on the boundary line with Burma and Captain Grant's Dispatches from Manipur are important. The North-East Frontier (NEF) Section gives a large range of archival information about the tribes of this region. The State Departments' Records give information relating to privy purse and settlement of private properties of the Princely States. The Military Records on the North-East Region is an important archival property. H.K. Barpujari Collection (1839–82) and Rajendra Prasad papers (1935–62) are worth mentioning for this region. Besides, the vernacular native newspapers of Eastern Bengal and Assam (1907–1911) including PRACHIN BANGLE PART SANKALAN—by S.N. Sen, (1942) may be mentioned. Aitchson's Collections, papers, relating to Rani Gaidinliu, and the Foreign and Political Department documents on the Kuki Rebellion are also very valuable.

The State Archive of Assam is keeping so many documents relating to Manipur. These are, now transferred to Manipur.

Institutions like the Anthropological Survey of India and The Asiatic Society have got a very rich collection of secondary sources. Five years back the Law Research Institute of the Gauhati High Court has brought out volumes on Land system of Manipur, Mizoram, Tripura, Meghalaya, Arunachal Pradesh and on Customary Laws and practices of the different tribes in North-East India. The volume on *Administration of Justice Among Tribes and Races of North-Eastern Region* may also be mentioned. The various Research organisations like the North-East India History Association (NEIHA), North-East India Council of Social Science Research (NEICSSR), have their published proceedings. The Manipur State Kala Academi, Manipur Folklore Society, The Directorate for the Development of Tribals and Backward Classes, Centre for Tribal Research of the Manipur University are some of the research promoters in this State.

Scripture: Manipur has very rich original scriptural property. In the Indian History Congress at Bombay University in 1980, a partial exhibition of the Manipur Scriptures was organised.

Bibliographies: The Select Bibliography of the North-East India, Bibliography of published material of this region are available in the National Library at Calcutta and the Anthropological Survey of India at Calcutta. The North-Eastern Council (NEC) and the Indian Council of Social Science Research—North-Eastern Regional Centre (ICSSR-NERC) have also compiled bibliography of published material. The Centre for Tribal Research, Manipur University has also published a bibliography pertaining to this area. N.E.H.U. has published Social Science Research—A select Bibliography, Nagaland, Arunachal Pradesh and Mizoram. A select Bibliography; Meghalaya, Manipur and Tripura. A Select Bibliography and dissertation North-East India: Humanities and Social Science.

Folkloric Material: The multi-contextual and inter-disciplinary value of folklore are accepted academically. The Manipur Government College (M.G.C.) Sub-Committee on the Promotion of Folklore Studies has recommended inter-disciplinary research. Manipur is rich in folk material. But the field of folklore is not yet fully organised. The Folklore Research Society of Manipur can at best be termed as a small beginning.

Material on Tribal Problems: Apart from the published source materials on the tribal socio-political problems, there is virtually no systematic source material available. It is a field where the task of the social science research becomes quite tough. No doubt, source materials are there, in the shape of Memorandum, Resolutions, Proceedings etc. And many other types of written records are there. But these are all stray materials. Many written materials on customary laws, folk songs, tales and so on often tempt the researchers. But the availability and accessibility becomes quite difficult. Materials that are kept in private custody of the individuals, leaders, social workers in the tribal society. They have to be made available through institutional help and patronisation.

The socio-political problems in the tribal societies of Manipur are in constant flux. In the last two decades we have found a great dynamism in the hill society, and politics. The material relating to these developments are to be made more systematic. In this connection, the Biographical materials may be searched out, if any and kept ready (with translations) for the use of scholars.

Scientific management of the source-material for interdisciplinary social science research on Manipur must be initiated. Social Science Data Bank is the most urgent need of the researchers. Different agencies, including the government departments and private individuals should make a coordination to enrich such Data Bank.

Target fixation in the 1990s is an urgent task. We are to take stock of the existing research material on social science and use the same for an inter-disciplinary study. Once the stock taking is done then we will be in a position to know where we are. Only then we will be able to help the researchers.

In the first part, several basic questions have been raised. Without going into the ideological contradictions that may be revealed in such questions, it can be safely concluded that what is needed is both conceptual efficiency and applicability (or relevance). The concept of Social Policy Research, though developed in America, may be made flexible so as to square up with the local situation. In an under-developed society like ours, we can hardly afford to compartmentalise pure Research and Social Policy Research in the literal sense of the term. The prioritisation of Pure-Research or social policy research in our context is not possible. The two areas should go hand in hand.

CHAPTER 2

Political Research

Every society has undergone many changes in the course of its history. The nature of these changes are influenced or determined by the level of social, economic and political development of the society. In a plural society like India, especially in North-East India, the nature of social, economic and political changes are in a criss-cross manner. This is mainly because of the diversities of the various communities. North-East India is said to have maximum diversity in India than in the whole world. The level of social, economic and political development in North-East India is some what lower as compared with other States of India. The late introduction of modern democratic processes and practices in the region may be a major factor for such low level of development. Though enjoying equal political status with other States of the Indian Union yet the States in the Northeast suffer from many drawbacks. As a result, many problems of diverse nature have developed. These problems cannot be solved haphazardly. It needs in-depth study of the problems, pointing out the various causes, impact and the future course of action. To-day our understanding of the social, economic and political systems and structures in North-East India, especially in Manipur, is very poor. How the society is undergoing change and in what direction different forces are pulling it are not properly understood. This calls for an unbiased research based on scientific methods, rising above personal or sectional interests. This will help social scientists to develop a right type of research in the right direction. This type of research can provide an effective link between theory and practice.

The following are some of the problems, which may be given priority in the conduct of research in Manipur.

TRADITIONAL POLITICAL SYSTEM AND MODERN POLITICAL INSTITUTIONS

There are 29 recognised tribes in Manipur. In addition, there are many unrecognised and sub-tribes. There are also backward communities such as Lois etc. In rural areas, each of the tribes or community has its own traditional political system. Some of these political systems have democratic elements, some are authoritarian and some are semi-monarchical. The introduction of modern democratic institutions such as Panchayats or District Councils within the framework of Indian constitution hardly affected the working of these traditional political institutions. Temporary adjustments, such as making the traditional chieftain or *khullakpa* the President of these elected democratic bodies has been made by the provisions of the various Acts passed by the State Government. But no proper adjustment has been made so far in the working of these bodies. Very few research works have been done in this area.

VOLUNTARY ORGANISATIONS AND THE POLITICS OF THE STATE

Groups play a very important role in the socio-political change of the state. Such is the role of voluntary organisations in Manipur. There are many voluntary organisations in the form of clubs, societies, and associations in Manipur. Most of them claim to be non-political in their respective constitutions.

There is always an indirect link between these voluntary organisations and the political process in the State. Most of these organisations take an active part in the electoral politics of the State. Both independents and party candidates vie with each other to establish closer links with these organisations in order to get themselves elected. These voluntary organisations, very often express their views on major political issues. Sometimes they also act as pressure groups on the government. Thus, in practice they do not always follow their constitutional provision of being non-political.

DEMAND FOR AUTONOMY

There are many ethnic groups in Manipur. Each group asserts for the protection of their ethnic identity. In the last stage, this assertion comes in the form of a demand for political autonomy. The Zeliangrong tribes of Manipur earlier demanded the creation of an autonomous administrative unit for them. At present, they are demanding that all Zeliangrong inhabited areas in the hills should be under one autonomous district. The Kukis are demanding the creation of an autonomous Kuki homeland. The Nagas, on the other hand, are demanding that the Naga inhabited areas in the hills of Manipur should be grouped together. Side-by-side the majority people of Manipur, i.e., the Meiteis are demanding that the name of Manipur should be changed to Kangleipak, the original name of Manipur.

POLITICAL PARTIES, BOTH NATIONAL AND REGIONAL

The growth of political parties in Manipur has been much delayed as compared with other State of India. In the working of parliamentary democracy, the political parties have to play a mature role. In addition to it, the political parties have also to educate the people politically. But it seems that the political parties are not producing desired and satisfactory result. For example, no political party secured a comfortable majority in the elections in order to form a stable government. Defections were very rampant before the enforcement of anti-defection law. And one witnessed factionalism, groupism, dissident politics, personality clashes etc. in the working of political parties after the enforcement of antidefection law. In the conduct of research, one should take into account the close relation between the socio-economic structure of the society and the political system.

WOMEN AND POLITICS IN MANIPUR

Manipur is essentially a women dominated society. When the society is characterised by social, economic and political instability women always come in the forefront. So the creation of political awareness and the inculcation of right political culture into the minds of women is very necessary for social, economic and political stability of the state. The social, economic and political values in the present Manipuri society have very much eroded.

As a result, many problems are cropping up. It would be worthwhile to conduct research in such areas like level of political consciousness and the professional women, political awareness and women, like market women, women and political parties, political participation of women etc.

To sum up, the areas which may be given priority from a political point of view in Manipur are interaction between the traditional political systems with modern political institutions, role of voluntary organisations in Manipur, working of political parties both national and regional, demand for autonomy, and women and politics in Manipur in general.

CHAPTER 3

Geographical Approach

Before making any observation on priorities in research, I would like to make a point. This indulgence in a semantic exercise may sound pedantic, but as this colloquium is being held in an academic environment and the bureaucracy is represented by a number of its luminaries, this indulgence does not seem to be out of place.

My question is—what priority the bureaucracy assigns to the research carried out by the academicians? A lot of research is being done in the Universities and their affiliates. Ph. D. and M. Phil. theses and project reports are being prepared every year. Are these being looked into by the administrators, planners and policy makers? Do they take any interest in knowing what researches are being done in the Universities, and what information or strategy can they provide in the formulation and implementation of their programmes and policies? If yes, then further discussion on priority in research can have any validity. Otherwise, how does it matter whether you are investigating into the variation of cephalic indices of the various tribal groups or into the impact of irrigation on their socio-economic well-being?

It is true that sometimes the government departments and government sponsored bodies initiate some type of research with a value to formulate some programmes or projects in keeping with their administration and planning. Sometimes academicians of the universities are also associated with such activities. My contention is that only such collaborative exercises in research can be of any use. It is the government, the policy makers, who can set the priorities in the field of research in which the academicians can collaborate and help.

It is nice that the organisers of this colloquium have brought both the bureaucracy and the academicians on a single platform to give a thought on the research priority for the State of Manipur. It is hoped that the participants from the government side could open their minds and spell-out the priorities they might have set, or might be setting for the period so that the academicians can lend their support by channelising their research activities in that direction.

I take upon myself the task of pointing out some lines along which geographers can contribute their might in meeting their objectives. The objective of any welfare government should be, according to the well-known Indian tradition yoga and kshema of the people, *i.e.*, acquisition of material wealth, and the preservation and improvement of the wealth so acquired. In the modern context it can be understood as development of all the means of production, and conservation/producing and production of resources; of and all these to be done in a planned manner; in other word planning for development and conservation.

In the context of the developing nature of the economy of the nation, and especially of the North-East, without any hesitation I am inclined to assert that over-emphasis on fundamental research in this region is a crime. Almost the entire research activity should be oriented towards applied side, that is, in making use of the knowledge, skill and expertise of the discipline in amelioration of the problems of the masses. That means, we should endeavour to channelise our research activities towards the improvement in the quality of life and social well-being of the people in a planned manner. This will, I think, quite fit into the planning policy of the government. Within this broad framework the following fields and sub-fields may be identified.

1. LEVELS OF DEVELOPMENT

One of the aims of planning is to correct or reduce the imbalances in development. This can be done only if we know what are the levels of development of the various units of administration—village or taluk or district. In the emphasis on village/block level planning it would be useful to know what is the level of development in each of the villages of the taluk or block, and categorise them on a five-point scale so that the development measures may be directed according to their needs. For district, the block should be categorised and for the whole North-Eastern region the districts should form the units for investigation. If such an exercise has been done earlier, another should be done now to see what changes have taken place since the time of the earlier study. This will provide both temporal and spatial perspective for plan implementation.

2. QUALITY OF LIFE

Another facet of the planning problem is the assessment of the quality of life, which can be done on village basis. Villages should be identified lacking in one or other amenities, which go to make life livable and happy.

3. HIERARCHY OF SETTLEMENTS

It is another facet of the planning process. The rural and the urban settlements are to be surveyed according to their functions. As a result of this, settlements can be identified as dependent villages, service centres, growth points, growth centres and growth poles. The functional gaps can be identified which will help in provision of the required function in the gap villages or areas. The growth facet can function as stimulants to growth and development in the area concerned.

4. RURAL SETTLEMENT STUDIES

Up till now a base study of settlements has not been done. There is a need to study the internal structure of these settlements as regards their spatial characteristic, social groupings and economic conditions. The use of land within the settlements (where they are compact) can be a useful study for planning for housing and social amenities.

5. LAND USE

Study of land use provides the baseline information for planning. Though this concept is in vogue for a long time, proper use has not been made of it. Land use survey may be done on village level. In the hilly and mountainous regions of the North-East the existing land use should be correlated with the slope, and land capability so that land use planning can be done to check soil deterioration and to improve productivity, and work towards environmental recuperation. Besides, changing carrying capacity should be calculated on a village to village basis to assess the changing relation between the people and their economy and to take remedial measures.

6. ADMINISTRATIVE BOUNDARIES

There has been very fast growth in the number of administrative units in the region. In the process even town and village units have been split causing a lot of socio-economic problems. What are the consequences of new boundary demarcations of the kind and what are its remedies? Such studies may form another fruitful direction of research.

7. IMPACT ASSESSMENT

Impact assessment can be categorised into two types:

(a) Impact of the planning process on the socio-economic life of the people. This will include the assessment of the degree of success or otherwise of the socio-economic measures taken under the five year plans such as the poverty-alleviation programmes or the Tribal Area Development programmes or the TRYSEM and so on. Spatial dimension of the plan implementation results may be mapped, discussed and remedial measures suggested.

(b) Impact on the Environment: North-East is an area of rich forest, aesthetic spots and historical monuments. What has the impact of the plans—like dams, reservoirs, extension of sedentary cultivations, industrial plants, human rehabilitation—on these natural and cultural elements, may be fruitful fields of investigation.

Several of these fields of study will be more rewarding if interdisciplinary approach is made, provided academicians make up their minds to do so by shaking off their bias against disciplines other than their own.

CHAPTER 4

Determining Research Priorities in Manipur

A systematic investigation to establish facts or causes or principles or to collect information on a subject or problem is called Research. In order to determine the priorities of Research in Manipur one has to see the relevance of the present day economic standard along with the socio-cultural and also the environmental problems of the inhabitants. All of us are well acquainted that the State of Manipur has been physiographically divided into three distinct zones viz., (i) The Hills, (ii) The plains and (iii) The Foothills. Comparatively, it is a small, remote and communicationally a backward zone of the country. It has been the home of the Meiteis, 29 sub-tribes belonging to Kuki and Naga groups, and a few other communities. The growth of population in the State has been continuously and alarmingly increasing on the limited land resources of the state. One of the most serious problems faced by the State is the rapidly increasing pressure of population on physical resources, particularly on land. The land area is fixed and inextensible while the population is increasing at a rate never before reached in the history of the State. With the increase in population, the per capita share of arable land decreases and consequently jhum cycle has been reduced to 2/3 years from 5/7 years 50 years ago in the hills. Consequently the vast forest area of the State has been reduced to microscopic patches -causing high rate of soil erosion and soil wash on the hill slopes while rapid siltation to the river beds, and drying of lakes and wetlands causing flash floods and droughts in the valley.

Despite hard labour, the total economic growth in the State is much below the natural level. Consequently, a large section of the population exist at a very low level of living. Further, it is also a fact that by 2000 AD Manipur will have 7.42 lakh unemployed. The State can provide for just 31 thousand posts only. In a State where the population pressure is continuously increasing upon extremely limited land resources, endless expansion of deforestation with adverse environmental degradation is taking place and unplanned growth of settlement is continuing, no peaceful and progressive condition can be expected. This may stimulate researchers to investigate the problems of State's Development and progress. This will concern different branches of knowledge, which directly concern the people of this state. The need for such researches becomes all the more imperative in the region like ours where the available land resource is limited, the productivity is low and more than 70 percent of the total population are directly dependent on agriculture.

The important holistic aspect of the State's problem is the determination of appropriate man-land ratio that would fit in with the optimum production of adequate foodstuff and other infrastructural requirements. Therefore, priority of the research area should be given to the studies of land use and its associated problems under the prevailing climatic, physiographic conditions and food habits of the people.

Secondly, researches are required to think of a change in the cropping or farming pattern of the state, particularly in the hills. However, any change should have to be economically and environmentally viable and should also be acceptable by the inhabitants of the area. In this case one may choose the problem of introduction and implementation of "Natural Farming" technique in the State.

Thirdly, most of the hill areas commonly practice the traditional techniques of farming with certain ethnic law concerning land-use, but due to the changing circumstances the system has collapsed. Therefore, sociologically one may think of studying the issue of ethnic law concerning Land use with the changing circumstances.

Fourthly, the impact of the environmental upheavals or uncertainties in the social context should also be investigated.

The detrimental effects of the Ithai Barrage, the deterioration of the fresh water body of Loktak lake and their effects on the life style, occupation as well as life-line of the people around the area pose a great threat to the very existence of the valley systems of the State. The ecological hazards to the people consequent to the construction of the Tipaimukh High Dam cannot be overlooked. The social invariability and occupational loss of about 10,000 people to be rendered homeless due to the inundation of 275 sq. km. of land area due to the construction of the High Dam should be given priority for investigation.

Lastly, the State Government has been taking up specific economic programmes for both the hills and the valley. However, specific economic planning of the foothill area is yet to be done. Therefore, research priority should also be given to the foothill areas of the State.

Considering the immediate problems of concern of the State the researches in the field of Social Sciences shall have to look into the above mentioned problem area as priority one. Any research in these areas shall have social and economic credibility. In a country like India where democratic form of government is existing, each and every individual citizen has his/her own right and duty to contribute to the cause of the development of their family, their locality, their society, state and nation. Therefore, research for research sake and degree only will not make a self-reliant country. Every individual research scholar shall have the courage to combat the problems of upliftment of the Society and Nation. Accordingly, funding agencies in the field of Social Science Research shall have to look into the above mentioned priority areas for funding. Only when the funding agencies implement as per the priority fixed in the context of the socio-economic and environmental relevance of the inhabitant the scholar will effectively share their contribution in making a self-reliant nation.

CHAPTER 5

Physiographical Approach

Economic development is the ultimate goal for all research activities. The success or failure of many research projects in the region is primarily subject to the topography or geographical situation of the project area.

The overall economic development of a particular area depends upon production and production management. But every effort should be aimed for the welfare of the people. The most important factor for project expansion and development is the minimum risks from infrastructural problems. Permanent infrastructural facilities depend upon the physiography of the area.

The present research problems are mostly focused on the application of science and technology. But the adoption of science and technology in the hilly region of the North-Eastern India faces major constraints because of the physiography itself. While considering the physiography for developmental research of the North-Eastern India, particularly of Manipur, the following characteristics are to be studied intensively: (a) Altitude and landscape, (b) Climate and Agro-climatic condition, (c) Soil and fertility, (d) Demography and population distribution, (e) Environment and natural resources, (f) Geographical continuity, and (g) Economic viability. If we examine Manipur from the above physiographic point of view the following important points appear to be the basis for research priority.

(i) There are high altitude areas with hills in Ukhrul and Mao areas. The remaining parts are hilly region with a small basin of the Imphal river in the centre. The slopes are of different degrees from place to place.

(ii) The State is under sub-tropical climate zone with heavy rainfall and short dry period. Agro-climatically, there are three important zones in the States: (a) Mild tropical area particularly at Moreh and Jiribam, (b) Sub tropical hill and plain area and (c) Temperate hill areas of Ukhrul, Mao and Tengnoupal ranges.

(iii) Soil erosion is common in the hills. And the cultivable fertile area is not suitable for large scale farming except for Animal Husbandry.

(iv) About nine-tenths of the area is occupied by backward tribal community with density of about 24 persons per sq. km. On the other hand, Imphal valley, with less than one-tenths of the state area, is densely populated with more than 200 persons per sq. km. Shifting cultivation and hunting are the occupation for hills and agriculture and fisheries are for the valley area. Most of the population are at subsistence level. Rice, vegetables, fish and meat are the important food items for the people.

(v) The important natural resources to be commercialised are, (a) Water resources, (b) Oak and tasar trees, (c) Cane and bamboos etc.

Large projects to be taken up are mainly power production from water resources. Small projects based on water harvesting are the points to be considered.

(vi) The economic relationship with other neighbouring areas should be considered. Research in production sector is necessary particularly for ensuring self-sufficiency of food, fuel power and energy.

Self-sufficiency in food introduction in rural area will be possible only through intensive research on rural technology for diversified farming, not through fully mechanised and specialised farming system depending upon the topography and landscape.

Research in adoption of suitable forest policy (fuel wood) without effecting the forest ecology is necessary for rural development.

Further, research in production of more power and energy mostly from the available water and solar resources are also one important priority for expansion of export based valued products in the state, *i.e.*, small-scale industries and handicrafts.

CHAPTER 6

Historical Perspective

This paper is an humble attempt to locate some of those areas in the history and culture of North-East India embracing all the three periods: ancient, medieval and modern to which priority can be accorded for carrying out researches in a broader perspective so as to present a comprehensive, comparative, objective, critical and analytical picture. The selected areas are given below:

1. ORIGINS, MIGRATIONS, SETTLEMENT PATTERNS, ETHNOLOGY AND ANTIQUITY OF THE TRIBAL PEOPLE

There is no denying that a host of scholars belonging to different disciplines have carried out their researches into this aspect of the subject during the last four decades, and earlier, but the picture which emerges from the researches carried out so far is neither graphic nor accurate. The views put forth by many scholars are no longer tenable. There is an imperative need to examine the historical authenticity of the conventional explanations of the racial classification theories which are full of fallacies and absurdities with particular reference to the Mongoloid origin of the tribal people of this region. No serious attempt has yet been made by any scholar to draw a clear-cut demarcation between the indigenous people or autochthones and emigrants, to determine their antiquity and to decide on the periods of migration and their settle-ments in different areas in the geographical setting within the chronological framework. All the relevant sources on the histories of ancient China, Burma, Tibet and South-East Asia, from the different parts of which the people concerned are supposed to have migrated, have not been thoroughly investigated. Many mysteries of history are yet to be unraveled. We still find ample scope for recasting the subject by adopting an interdisciplinary approach to the study of the problems concerned. The anthropological, ethnological, philological, archaeological, literacy and historical data are yet to be harmonized by striking a reasonable balance between them as well as with meticulous regard for the truth. This is, indisputably, one of the areas in the realm of social science research which deserves priority.

2. ARCHEOLOGICAL RESEARCH

The history of this region still lies buried in archaeological perspective. The archaeological research is still in its infancy. All the salient features of the Paleolithic, Neolithic and Chalcolithic phases of the tribal cultures are yet to be discovered by linking them up with the contemporary phases of ancient Indian history and civilization. The study of regional history in this regard should always be viewed as more complementary than contradictory to that of Indian history. There is still a great need for undertaking an archeological exploration and excavation of the sites concerned for rediscovering the past. The antiquity of the archeological finds needs to be ascertained by employing the carbon-dating method for which facilities are available in the physical research laboratories in Ahmedabad. The subject also offers a wide scope for making a comparative study of the megalithic culture of this region and that of Southern India and South-East Asia.

The study of art, architecture, sculpture and iconography comparing and contrasting all the prominent eastern schools of art has not yet attracted the serious attention of researchers. The contributions made by the people of this region in different fields of art in general and to the evolution of artistic culture of India in particular have not yet been sufficiently highlighted.

3. POLITICAL AND CULTURAL CONTACTS

The mutual political and cultural contacts between the people of Assam, Manipur and Tripura as well as their contacts with neighbouring kingdoms like Bengal, Bihar and Orissa through the ages effecting the traditional religion, art, culture, language and literature also deserve our notice.

4. HINDUISM AND BUDDHISM

The rise and growth of Hinduism with reference to the Saiva, Sakti and Tantric cults and other faiths and that of Buddhism particularly in the tribal areas still await historical treatment at the hands of researchers. The circumstances and factors leading to the rise of Buddhism in Arunachal Pradesh, Manipur and Tripura in Ancient and Medieval period are yet to be analysed within the wide canvass.

5. TRIBAL REPUBLICS

The age-old republican institutions of the tribal people of this region have not yet been studied in detail in comparison to ancient Indian tribal republics.

6. TRADE AND COMMERCE

The sources dealing with internal and external trade and commerce of the tribal people of this region in general and with commercial intercourse with far distant countries like China and Rome have also not been undertaken so far.

7. THE ROLE OF THE TRIBAL PEOPLE IN THE REPULSION OF THE MUSLIM INVASIONS

The role played by the people of the plains and valleys of Assam in repulsing the successive attacks of the Muslims made altogether sixteen or seventeen times between 1206 and 1680 A.D. for extending their imperial authority have already been brought to light by the local scholars of Assam and other distinguished historians of India. But the contributions which the tribal people of this region made in frustrating their attempt of planting the banner of crescent over the political horizon of North-East India are still wrapped up in obscurity. It is worthy to note that the heroic sacrifices which they made, constitute an addition to the saga of bravery displayed by their compatriots of other regions of India. The subject has not received due treatment at the hands of scholars.

8. TRIBAL RENAISSANCE

There is a fair scope for undertaking research in the history of the political awakening of the tribal people for the revival of their traditional religion and culture.

9. THE REVOLT OF 1857

The roles played by the people of this region in the revolt of 1857, also known as first Indian war of Independence, are yet to be evaluated. The study of the subject will definitely help us fill in several gaps in our existing knowledge about the subject in the Indian context.

10. ANTI-BRITISH TRIBAL MOVEMENTS AND THE FREEDOM STRUGGLE

The role played by the tribal people in the anti-British movement from 1828 to 1942 with special reference to the participations of some section of them in the Indian struggle for freedom can be assessed only by further research on the subject.

CHAPTER 7

Environmental Research

Environmental sciences deal with processes and phenomena of nature which provide resources and conditions for development of man and his society. Their aim consists in comprehending and predicting the pattern of interactions and phenomena leading to social, cultural, economic growth and development of human societies.

Our society is facing many challenging problems. The decrease in vegetal cover, erosion of soil, siltation of reservoirs, decline in land productivity, and incidents of flood and drought are some of them. Thus, in research projects man-nature relationship is to be formulated taking into account people's environmental behaviour. Researches in environmental sciences should not be diagnostic but should aim at projecting a normative model for our society for suitable environmental behaviour and resource management.

All research projects in environmental sciences of the region must reflect the endogenous creation for efficient use of ecosystems for eco-development (eco-development consists in stimulating local initiatives for sound development of area or region) and should not be approved only for academic purpose. There is a need for greater linkage between scientific researches and community at large. It is more relevant particularly in case of environmental sciences.

The approach in environmental researches should be inter or multi-disciplinary, but the teaching and research in itself has to be discipline based. Hence, fundamental and environmental researches are not contradictory terms. As one knows that specialists can work best in their laboratories where they can interact with the co-workers in University departments. But we have to provide them opportunities for meaningful dialogue and thus organisational requirement for environmental studies and researches. Ecological understanding binds several disciplines, the emphasis being on the network of relationships, *i.e.*, ecology. Through ecology one learns the principles essential for evolution of man and biosphere. It can also bring about ethical and intellectual changes in attitude, which can reverse the natural and cultural degradations.

In order to decide how to go in for studies and researches, we may analyse the various components of environment like physical, chemical, biological, social, cultural etc., each of which can be taken up as a project in research programmes and then discovering the nature of their dynamic interrelationships. For example, intensive agricultural practices in hills have affected the soil and water since ages which has resulted in low productivity, erosion of top soil, siltation of reservoirs, flood problem etc. The problem is to be addressed from different angles involving different disciplines is to be considered. The environmental problems are to be solved with proper understanding of disciplines—like modern management science, systems analysis, simulation modeling, behavioural sciences, decision theory, pollution monitoring, urban design and operational research.

A research worker (who has been trained in a particular discipline), who is working on environmental problem should be given general short term courses on Environmental Sciences and special detailed courses on the types of problems with which he has to deal with. It is essential to impart such Environmental Education to the researcher that enables him to become a committed participant in planned implementation of measures for preserving and improving the environment. It is equally important to disseminate knowledge to those who in different ways interact with the environment and can modify it. It must be the concern of ecologist to educate common people on ecological problems so that they realise the gravity of problems and co-operate for a better tomorrow.

The collaborative research programmes in environmental sciences must be based on—

a) Ecosystem Evaluation—(assessing the characteristics of the eco-system in terms of relevant to physical, economic and social context of the area and analysing resource availability on a suitable basis without degrading or polluting the environment).
b) Assessment of Environmental Effects—(identifying, predicting, interpreting and communicating information about effects of an action—be it a policy, programme, legislation, proposal, engineering project of other operation with environmental implications).
c) Using Allocations—(preparing resource inventory and maps of ecosystem, allocating resources on basis of current and projected patterns of demand for development programmes and giving consideration to demand and energy settlement patterns).

Concurrently with ecosystem evaluation and using allocations, collaborative research programmes on eco-development of the states must be taken. The projects pertaining to region must involve ecosystem in the neighbourhood and impact of human activities on their structure and functioning. The available human resources of the states must be channelised and funding agencies should provide monetary assistance for such works.

The projects for collaborative research programmes in the region may be classified as:

1. Based on local needs
2. Based on community needs (of direct relevance) and
3. Theoretical, experimental and field studies on sequential effects in space and time which need environmental monitoring

1. Based on local needs—
   a) Low cost sanitation, both rural and urban, compatible with local ecosystems.
   b) Suitable cropping and land use pattern with special reference to hills region.
   c) Harnessing non-conventional energy resources in local eco-planning and development programming and encouraging women to use technologies for energy consumptions.

2. Based on Community needs (Direct Relevance)—
   a) Water pollution.
   b) Flood management.

3. Theoretical, Experimental and Field studies
   a) Conservation, management and improvement of (a) wild life, forests, lakes and national parks, and (b) to evaluate interaction between Keibul Lamjao National park and Human Settlements around.
   b) Assessment of short and long term consequences of human intervention such as urbanisation, construction of roads, bridges, dams, intensive agricultural practices etc. (like problem of landslides).
   c) Soil conservation in catchment areas.
   d) Reclamation of waste lands and wet lands for agriculture, forestry, fishery etc.

CHAPTER 8

Export Potential of Manipuri Handloom Products and its Economic Implications for the State

In the textile industry the handloom sector has enjoyed its unique status. This is especially true in the case of Manipur. Now what have begun to emerge at the national scene is the growing exports of this ancient cottage industry. Cotton handloom exports alone rose from the value of Rs. 11 crores in 1966 to over Rs. 400 crores in 1992. These products flowed to nearly 150 countries spread over all the continents. Observers of the industry have predicted that this trend is bound to grow and the potential can be exploited through proper marketing.

The Central Government on its part is showing considerable concern for this sector. In 1985 it passed the handloom Industries Act and recently the Supreme Court has reserved 22 items for exclusive production by the handloom sector alone. Both the Handloom Export Processing Council (HEPC) Madras and National Handloom Development Corporation (NHDC) Lucknow, are rendering service to this industry. Though the handloom weavers are in the unorganised sector and under the cooperative fold, many of them are adopting a professional approach to gain both distinctive competence and competitive advantage in the global market. They have developed products in keeping with international demand and taste, followed pricing strategies to beat the competition, evolved distribution logistics at par with the best in the industry and have initiated and sustained promotional campaigns to create international awareness of the unique features of their products resulting in increased customers for their goods.

It is hypothesised that if Indian handlooms have done so well in the international market, there is every possibility that Manipuri handlooms of the same country will do equally well if not better. This hypothesis, however, needs to be tested and that is where the research problem arises. Research will have to be done on the present and potential buyers of Indian handloom products. For this the present exporters may be contacted. Besides, HEPC provides funds for, as well as organises, buyer seller meets. It also provides funds to handloom cooperatives and individual weavers to attend international trade fairs organised in the country and abroad. In these trade fairs handloom products are exhibited and feed back is obtained based on either purchases made or comments, observations or suggestions received. HEPC also does research on its own and they may help researchers working on the exports of Manipuri handlooms. Influential opinion makers from abroad are invited to inspect and learn about Indian handloom and later go back to their country and create favourable public opinion of our products. Many of these benefits can be taken advantage of.

AREAS TO BE RESEARCHED

1. Study and explore the possibilities of determining target markets.
2. Analyse the cost structure in order to minimise costs to make Manipuri handlooms price competitive internationally.
3. Explore the various sources of funds to reach global markets.
4. Unravel the means for popularising Manipuri handlooms abroad taking advantages of all available opportunities.
5. Taking assistance of export agents/middle men, at least initially, to reach markets abroad.
6. Examine the scope of computer aided design to make Manipuri handlooms go high-tech.

CHAPTER 9

Research Priorities—Economics (I)

The issue of priorities in Social Science research emerges as a result of our realization that social science research should be more sensitive to social issues and that the resources at our disposal in terms of finance, technical expertise and time have become grossly inadequate for the social problems in this region. The frequency and growing intensity of social upheavals to which this region has been subjected have disrupted the process of change. Besides a big question mark has appeared on the credibility of the direction of change and the institutions through which change is to be brought about. In other words the issue of priorities is intricately linked with the issue of relevance in social science research. Commenting on the twin needs of requirement of academic freedom and reflection of social reality in research V.K.R.V. Rao once remarked as follows:

"Research, whether in the natural or social sciences, is so much dependent on personal choice and personal commitment that it is some what rash to attempt laying down conditions that would circumscribe its scope or limit the freedom of the researcher. But the world in which we are functioning, where research is financed by public expenditure and thus in the last analysis by the people at large, it is difficult to escape some measures of social responsibility for the research work one undertakes. This is even more so for social science research, where results do not pass the same test as in natural sciences, where the problems involved rouse emotional responses and where the personal bias of the researcher is as important a factor in the choice of the project as in the results he seeks to find".

A social scientist seeks to develop models for the social reality of which he himself is a part and at the same time is accountable to the society for the uses of his knowledge which is a social product. Relevancy is synonymous with formulation of policy prescriptions for the problems confronting the society. It includes various factors and insights that help in the formulation of policies in the social and economic fields. In seeking relevance in social science research, one should not be unduly influenced by the requirements of the policy maker who generally has a short term outlook. Society functions on a continuum of time. Temporary solutions for today's problems normally fail to incorporate their repercussions on the problems of tomorrow or the possibilities of solving them. The long term and the multi-dimensional causes and consequences are relevant aspects of social science research which unfortunately get neglected. What is needed is policy based on a realistic conception of the prevailing conditions. It is also true that conceptions about reality are influenced by the interest of the dominant and articulate group in the society and the conceptions have a tendency to deviate from truth in a direction consistent with these interests. In the words of Myrdal "There is a tendency for all knowledge, like all ignorance, to deviate from truth in an opportunistic direction".

Having digressed on the issue priorities determined by social relevancy, let me comment on the current social science literature on the North-East especially in economics which is my discipline. That we have failed to join the mainstream meaning fully in the process of economic development is an indicator of our failure to delineate the dimensions of an economic policy which can arouse the dormant growth potential in this region. While highly technical and analytical studies are based on categories which are singularly inadequate for the realities of this area with the element of relevancy missing, other promising and relevant researches have suffered from lack of vigor and analytical frame work. Developing suitable categories is a big challenge before every social scientist. This mismatch is made more acute by the condescending attitude of mainland economists. While there is vociferous protest against the imposition of western prototypes on Indian realities, not much thought has been given to the adequacy or otherwise of the 'Indian Proto-types' for explaining the social realities of the North-East. Of late, there is a welcome tendency to switch over to data based research from the earlier descriptive research. However, a critical analysis of the data in terms of their conceptual adequacy and mode of collection reveals that there is room for improvement.

It is also not surprising that in spite of the much talked about Five Year Plan and its components specifically designed for the weaker sections of this region economic development has not percolated through its social strata. The consumption pattern is neither sustainable nor consistent with optimum utilisation of local resources. The absence of any well-conceived economic plan for any of the regions of North-East India capable of the harnessing and using optimally the available local resources is a sorry commentary on the status of economic research and also a poor reflection on the sense of priority of social scientists, take for instance, the case of Manipur. At the end of a series of plans since attaining statehood the state is hopelessly dependent on central doles and has utterly failed in developing any base for resource mobilisation. The government response to the current financial crisis was to raise the taxes on the ground that they have not risen in the last few years. No where do we find any mention of the question of their effects on work-incentives. It is as if we were operating on the rising segment of the Laffer Curve. Of course, our questions are a measure of our maturity and our failure is mainly due to the fact that we have not put the right question to ourselves. The competence for asking the right questions can not be attained without the support of other disciplines, e.g., history, sociology, social psychology and political science etc.

This more or less settles the question of priority in research methodology. We should adopt inter-disciplinary approach. As Gerschem Kron has rightly pointed out:

> "The quality of understanding of current problems largely depends on the broadness of the frame of reference."

In other words, uni-disciplinary approach involves insularity, which is a limitation on Comprehension. In the words of V.K.R.V. Rao:

> "An integrated approach that covers both the long and the short period and the associated components of social phenomena, including backward and forward linkages and a multi-disciplinary approach that reflects the role of many social sciences that influence human behavior becomes relevant when using social science research for formulating policy prescriptions."

Inter-disciplinary study is not the samething as saying that everything depends on everything else. It is an approach in which different disciplines can interact. The objective is to identify the causal system and it is not necessary that each and every variable should be included.

On the issue of priority in social science research I will comment again on issues mainly in economics not because of any conviction about their predominance but because of my familiarity with them. Top priority should be given to comprehensive inter-disciplinary studies on the resource base of this region. Some relevant questions may be as follows:

1. What is the quantum at our disposal?
2. How has it evolved over time?
3. Is it being used optimally?

The studies on resources should be extended to potential resources also. Any development plan not based on the local resources is doomed from the very beginning. The positive contributions, if any, are not sustainable. The formulation of development plans consistent with the local resources is a big challenge for the social scientists. The second priority should be accorded to agriculture, which has a predominant role in terms of its contribution to state domestic product and employment of the work force. However, it has become associated with low productivity and over-crowdedness. It conjures up an image of a jhumia or a farmer operating with rudimentary tools. In the case of Manipur it has been found that majority of the operational holdings come under the marginal and small category. Not all the components of new agricultural technology is size-neutral. While use of fertilizer and HYV seeds can be considered as size-neutral, the use of irrigation facilities and mechanisation are related to size. It means that the agrarian structure stands in the way of the farmers' reaping optimum benefits from the new technology. Besides, the gains of small farmers are further dissipated by their adverse terms of participation in the market. The effect of the technology on the soil is untouched. Here the question of appropriate technology arises. It needs to be seen whether we have adopted the most appropriate and sustainable agricultural technology. Are we following an activity-mix capable of maximum income generation subject to minimal adverse distributional and employment implications? These are serious questions for a polity torn apart by inequality and poverty. Why should a marginal farmer remain tied to mono-cropping with complete certainty about the inadequacy of his produce to meet his requirements directly and via the market? Land and labour need not be most efficiently used only in the production of food grains. Take the case of the jhumias whom we have failed to wean away from the practice of shifting cultivation. They have their own survival-related rationale. It is futile to try to make them switch over to settled cultivation until we succeed in influencing their perceptions of the objective conditions. If we fail to do so, it is better to devise ways and means to minimise their adverse consequences and nurture the elements of dynamism in the practice. It may even prove to be a strategy which the tribals can identify themselves with. The elements of continuity and sense of identification are important aspects of any policy.

The third priority should be given to demographic studies questions about the demographic profile of the indigenous people of this region have become very pertinent because they invariably provide the basis for most of the social upheavals in this region. The issue of foreigners is capable of toppling any democratically elected government at any time. So far we have been shying away from a frontal attack on this problem. It will be worthwhile to examine the factors which have shaped our response in their totality. It will also be worthwhile to analyse the economy and implications of this human phenomenon. If we are not able to push them back, it will be more worthwhile to evolve policy measures, which not only enable them to contribute fully to the regional economy but also minimise the adverse implications.

In the preceding sections I have tried to identify the priorities of research in economics for this region on the basis of their social relevance. My order need not be 'the order'. However, the question of their consistency with the order in other social sciences is beyond the scope of this paper and is better left to those who can.

REFERENCES

Gerschen Kron, A., *Economic Backwardness in Historical Perspective*, Harvard University Press, Cambridge, 1962.

Myrdal, G., *The Challenge of World Poverty*, Penguin Books, 1970.

Rao, V.K.R.V., "Introductory, The problem of Relevance in Social Science Research" in Institute of Economic Growth, *Relevance in Social Science Research: A Colloquium*, New Delhi, 1982.

CHAPTER 10

Research Priorities—Economics (II)

North-Eastern India comprises of 7 (seven) states, viz., Arunachal Pradesh, Assam, Manipur, Meghalaya, Mizoram, Nagaland and Tripura. It has a total area of 255083 sq. km. comprising 7.76 percent of the total geographical area of the country (3,287,263 sq. km.). But for the small strip connecting Assam and Bengal it is almost isolated geographically. Except for the Brahmaputra Valley, Imphal Valley and some valley areas of Tripura the rest are of hills. Therefore, in totality the entire region can be described as hilly region.

The region has a total population of 3,138,6911 as per 1991 Census. This constitutes 3.71 percent of the total population of the country (844,324,222). The density of population per sq. km. of area is only 123 against 265 for all India.

Economically, the region as a whole is very backward. Except for a few large and medium industries in the Brahmaputra valley there is hardly any other large and medium industries in the rest of the region. Only 83.82 percent of the villages are electrified as on March 1992. Agriculture continues to be the back-bone of the economy of the region. Of the total gross cropped area of 4729 thousand hectares, only 491 thousand hectares are irrigated. This constitutes only about 11.58 percent. Only about 1/4th of the gross cropped area is under high yielding varieties.

In transport and communication too, the level of development is not satisfactory. The density of road per 100 sq. km. of area for the North-Eastern Region as on 31.3.89 is only

32.13 km. as against 47.23 km, for all India (ref. page 97, Basic Statistics of NER 1992, NEC). The income of most of the States of this region is poor. Therefore, these States cannot meet their budgetary requirements from their own resources. These seven States are treated as Special Category States for the purpose of plan financing. Because of the various factors including poverty, unemployment, etc. there is law and order problem in almost all the states.

Considering the above situation, some of the areas which can be considered for detail in-depth study may be as follows:

PHYSICAL RESOURCES OF THE REGION

Land, mineral wealth, water, forest, animal, plants, etc., the scope of the study may include the extent to which these resources can be economically exploited without unduly disturbing the eco-system.

LAND USE PATTERN

The trend/pattern of changes in the use of land for various purposes over a period of time, merit and demerit of the present land use system, the pattern/type of ownership and its impact, legal aspect, suggestion, etc.

PLANNING PROCESS

The state of economy, the quantum of investment in the various five year plans, the type of priorities given, the various physical targets, the achievements made, objectives and strategies adopted, the system of monitoring and evaluation, pattern of financing, etc.

RESOURCES

Tax base, tax structure, the rate of taxes, change in the rate of taxes, tax evasion, the scope for increase in the rate of taxes, cost of collection, income for taxes, etc.

PERFORMANCES OF THE PUBLIC SECTOR UNDERTAKINGS

The investment made, the assets created, income generated, loss and profit, reason for making loss or profit, scope for future improvement and expansion, scope for wielding up, scope for privatisation, problem for future funding etc.

INDUSTRIAL POTENTIAL

The present level of industrial development, raw materials available, the scope for expansion and establishment of new industries, areas to which priorities to be given, source of fund, etc.

POWER

Existing power available from various sources, the cost of present power generation, the cost of transmission and distribution, expenditure and income, losses of power in transmission and distribution, power potential available, taking up of power projects as a commercial venture, source of finance and technology, etc.

TRANSPORT

Various modes of transport available, road network available, railway network, area-wise availability of transport facility, transport and other activities, transport bottleneck, the cost of extending transport facility, the impact of transportation facility created, etc.

BUDGETS

The trend, composition of the budget, viz., plan and non plan, constituent/composition of plan and non-plan provision, the distribution between developmental and non-developmental expenditure, the ration of non-developmental expenditure to developmental expenditure, financing of the budget, present financial situation, etc.

All these aforesaid priority areas need to be looked into afresh and studied properly and methods for improvement be suggested on the basis of such scientific studies.

CHAPTER 11

Recommendations

In course of the panel discussion there emerged a near unanimity on at least two points in regard to the general approach of research on Manipur. These are:

i. In view of the urgent need for accelerating the developmental process in the region, priority should be given to applied research rather than on fundamental research, and
ii. In view of the multi-faceted nature of most of the problems of the region emphasis should be placed on inter- or multi-disciplinary research; without, however, side tracking the uni-disciplinary ones.

In keeping with the consensus, the topics listed below for priority research, though grouped under separate disciplines, should not be considered confined to the respective discipline, rather any topic can be considered under any discipline, provided an inter- or multi-disciplinary team is going to be involved in a proposed research.

LIST OF TOPICS

Anthropology

1. Folklore studies for discovering the commonality of interests between the various tribal groups as well as between the tribal and non-tribal population.
2. Relationship between the tribal customary laws, political system, and the modern laws,

3. Contribution of the region in the field of tribal arts.
4. Tribal ecological knowledge, resource rights and health issues.

Commerce

4. Exploration of target markets: both domestic and foreign—for handloom and handicraft products in identifying potential consumers.

Economics

5. Existing financial situation of the states in the region as a means to secure viability.
6. Tenancy and taxation structure to find ways to build local financial resources.
7. Impact of planning process especially geared to target achievement.
8. Economic facets of immigration especially to assess its possible contribution to the national economy.

Environmental Studies

9. Environmental studies to protect the ecosystem in view of developmental processes.

Geography

10. Land use survey for resource inventory as a basis for planning.
11. Levels of development—village, block and district levels.
12. Quality of life survey to plan provision of basis amenities.
13. Industrial potentials.
14. Transport accessibility and into bottleneck, and impact of new transport lines.
15. Settlement hierarchy to find service centres , growth points and growth centres.
16. Feasibility of mini-power projects and non-conventional sources of energy.
17. Boundary studies, both internal and inter-State.

History

18. Tribal renaissance for revival of traditional religion and culture.
19. Tribal republics of antiquity.
20. Politico-cultural contacts of the local people with neighbouring states and foreign countries.
21. Chronology of migration and settlement of various tribal groups in the region.

Political Science

22. Role of voluntary organisation in the politics of the states.
23. Functioning of political parties—regional and national in the region.
24. Role of women in the politics of the states of the region; and
25. Reason for demands for autonomy/or secession.